WHAT DO YOU KNOW ABOUT

PUBERTY AND GROWING

Pete Sanders and Steve Myers

28 JUN 2018

This edition published in 2000
© Aladdin Books Ltd 1995

Designed and produced by
Aladdin Books Ltd
28 Percy Street
London W1P 0LD

First published in
Great Britain in 1995 by
Franklin Watts
96 Leonard Street
London EC2A 4XD

Previously published in
hardcover in the series
Let's Discuss

ISBN: 0 7496 2093 5 (hardback)
ISBN: 0 7496 3814 1 (paperback)

A catalogue record for this
book is available from the
British Library.

Printed in Belgium

Designer   Tessa Barwick
Editor   Sarah Levete
Illustrators Mike Lacy
              Liz Watkins
Picture research Brooks Krikler
              Research

Pete Sanders is Senior Lecturer
in health education at the
University of North London.
He was a head teacher for
ten years and has written
many books on social issues
for children.

Steve Myers is a freelance
writer who has co-written
other titles in this series and
worked on several educational
projects for children.

The consultant, Dr Diana Birch,
MMBS DCH MRCP Msc MFCH
MD, is Director of Youth
Support. She works extensively
with young people.

Contents

HOW TO USE THIS BOOK

The books in this series are intended to help young people to understand more about personal issues that may affect their lives. Each book can be read alone, or together with a parent, teacher or helper, so that there is an opportunity to talk through ideas as they come up. Issues raised in the storyline are explored in the accompanying text, inviting further discussion.

At the end of the book there is a chapter called "What Can We Do?" This section provides practical ideas which will be useful for both young people and adults, as well as a list of the names and addresses of organisations and helplines, which offer further information and support.

−1− Introduction

In the story, Peter Pan refused to grow up. In real life, however, we are not given the choice. Puberty is a part of this process of change and development which happens to everyone.

Growing up is an exciting experience. It does have its challenges, and there can be problems to face, especially during puberty. This book helps you to understand about the physical and emotional changes that happen during puberty. It discusses the issues that growing up can raise for young people and adults. Each chapter introduces a different aspect of the subject, illustrated by a continuing storyline. The characters in the story deal with situations which many young people experience. By the end, you will know more about what growing up means and how it can make you feel.

Growing And Changing

Life is about change. From the moment we are born, we are constantly growing and developing, both physically and emotionally. Growing up means changing from a child, dependent upon others, to an independent adult. Part of this process involves changes to our bodies. Becoming an adult is also about gradually taking responsibility for your own life and forming your own views and attitudes about the world you live in.

Learning how to cope with, react to and adjust to change is a vital part of the process of growing up.

As you grow up, you become more responsible for yourself, and sometimes for others.

You only have to think about yourself as you were when you were a helpless, tiny baby and compare this with the way you are now, to realise how many changes you have already experienced. Some happen quickly. Others happen very gradually. Not all changes are immediately obvious. They may affect only the inside of your body or they might not change the body physically at all – for instance, learning how to talk, or understanding how to solve a maths problem. Some changes will be easy to cope with, especially if you know what is going to happen. Even so, having the facts about what to expect is only half the story. Growing up also means coming to terms with these new thoughts and feelings and learning how to express them.

There are two periods in a person's life when there are many changes all happening at once. One of these is the first two years of life, when babies learn how to walk, talk and make sense of the world around them. The other time of rapid growth and change is during 'puberty'.

LOTS OF PEOPLE SHARE MATTHEW'S WORRIES ABOUT THEIR BODY.

Some believe that their worth as a person is decided by how they look. This is not the case. Who we are is not just about our outward appearance – it is about the whole person: our personality, how we act and the way we feel about ourselves and other people.

Although we have many things in common, each of us is very different. Growing up is about learning how to enjoy and be proud of who you are.

THE MEDIA OFTEN PRESENT ONE KIND OF LOOK AS BEING BETTER THAN ANOTHER.

Many people have been persuaded to try to copy the images they see on TV and in advertisements. But there is no such thing as a 'perfect' body or look.

CASE STUDY:
SELINA, AGED 11

"I used to worry so much about how I looked. All the models in magazines looked so perfect. It was quite difficult when I was about 10 because my body seemed all out of proportion and I felt so awkward. But at school we talked about the physical changes that happen as you grow up. It's just the body's way of developing and it all evens out in the end. Besides, no one body is the same. What's important is to look after your body by eating well and taking enough exercise. You can't change your body's frame – so you might as well feel comfortable with it!"

Puberty – What Is It?

Puberty can be a time of confusion. It can feel as if your body is rebelling against you! But this physical and emotional upheaval is perfectly normal.

Once puberty begins you have begun the journey towards adulthood. Puberty happens to everyone. It is the body's way of preparing for the responsibilities of becoming an adult. This includes making the physical changes necessary for a person to be able to have sex and to have children. Puberty can begin up to two years before any physical changes are noticeable.

Diagrams which explain the physical changes you will experience as you grow up, do not always prepare you for the feelings that you may also have.

Nobody knows exactly what triggers off the process of puberty. There is no fixed age at which it will start or finish. It can depend on factors such as family history, the food you eat and your general state of health.

The changes that happen during puberty are the result of substances called 'hormones' which are released by a gland in the skull called the 'pituitary gland'. As well as causing the body to change physically, these hormones are also responsible for a range of emotions and feelings – some of which may be totally new to you. Learning to understand these feelings is a part of growing up.

▽ The following Monday, Mrs Green noticed that Matt seemed in a hurry to get to school.

WE'RE DOING 'GROWING AND CHANGING' WITH MR BUCKLEY. I THINK MY INNOCENT LITTLE BROTHER'S AFRAID OF MISSING SOMETHING.

NO I'M NOT. I JUST DON'T WANT TO BE LATE FOR SCHOOL, THAT'S ALL.

YOU DIDN'T HAVE TO SAY ANYTHING TO MUM. YOU'RE JUST AS CURIOUS AS I AM.

YES, BUT WHAT'S THE BIG DEAL? I KNOW MOST OF IT ALREADY.

△ Matt's mum and dad had always been open, but he still wanted to know more.

▽ In class, Mr Buckley described some of the changes that would happen as they grew older.

I HEARD THAT, SIR, MATTHEW JUST SWORE.

YOU'RE SUCH A TELL-TALE MICHELLE.

YOU'RE ALWAYS SWEARING.

▽ Matt burst into tears and was too embarrassed to speak.

▽ Michelle denied this. She, Adam and Matt began to argue.

OK, CALM DOWN ALL OF YOU. MATT, YOU SEEM TO HAVE A LOT ON YOUR MIND. WHY DON'T YOU TELL US ALL WHAT YOU KNOW ABOUT THE CHANGES BOYS GO THROUGH DURING PUBERTY?

HE'S STILL A KID, SIR. HE DOESN'T KNOW ANYTHING YET.

▽ Mr Buckley said that he had set up a 'suggestion box' so that they could write down any questions they had.

AND YOU'RE SO GROWN UP, I SUPPOSE. LEAVE HIM ALONE, JIMMY.

OK, CLASS, SETTLE DOWN. I KNOW SOME OF YOU FIND THIS DIFFICULT TO TALK ABOUT, BUT IT'S VERY IMPORTANT THAT YOU KNOW ABOUT IT.

DO WE HAVE TO PUT OUR NAMES ON?

NO. THAT WAY YOU SHOULDN'T FEEL EMBARRASSED ABOUT ASKING. WHATEVER WORRIES OR QUESTIONS COME UP, WE CAN DISCUSS AS A WHOLE CLASS.

THE AGE AT WHICH PUBERTY BEGINS VARIES FROM PERSON TO PERSON.

For some, it can be as early as eight years old. Others start around ten or twelve. Many may not start until their teenage years. It can be upsetting if you think everyone else has started, and you are feeling left behind. Or, if you have started puberty early, you might feel awkward and isolated from your friends. Situations like these can be hard to accept. It helps to remember that everyone goes through puberty at different stages.

THE CHANGES WHICH HAPPEN DURING PUBERTY ARE VERY PERSONAL.

Like Matt, both children and adults may feel embarrassed discussing them. Learning how to overcome this embarrassment and to talk about your feelings will help.

CASE STUDY:
FAROUK: AGED 13

"I kept wondering if I was normal. Although I thought I knew what to expect, I had these strange feelings and my body seemed to have a life of its own. I wanted to talk to somebody about it, but I thought mum and dad were too old to understand. I didn't want to ask my friends in case they made fun of me. In the end, I spoke to my older brother. He joked a bit at first, but then he told me that he'd felt the same when he was my age. Then I talked to a couple of my friends. I think they were secretly relieved to have someone to discuss their own feelings with."

Physical Changes In Girls

Some physical changes during puberty are similar for boys and girls, but others happen to one sex only.

The process of becoming a woman involves a series of physical changes, some of which you may not notice. For girls, the most significant physical changes are the development of breasts, and the beginning of 'menstruation' – having periods. Periods are not something to be afraid of, nor are they 'dirty'. Only women have periods, but boys should know what they are too.

During puberty, the egg-producing organs – 'ovaries' – inside the female body start to release eggs. The lining of the uterus, where a baby would grow if the egg were fertilised, thickens. During a period, this lining and the unfertilised egg are released because they are not needed. This whole process is known as the 'menstrual cycle'.

Most girls experience an increase in the amount of fat on their bodies. This means that some girls will put on some weight. There will also be an increase in height and the size of hands and feet. Head hair may become thicker and hair may grow on other parts of the body, particularly the pubic area and under the arms.

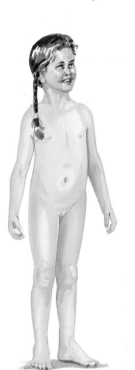
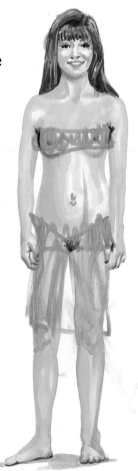

▽ A few weeks later, Suzanne was in the bathroom, when Jeremy burst in.

DO YOU MIND! DON'T YOU EVER KNOCK?

YOU'RE ALWAYS IN HERE, LOOKING AT YOURSELF. IT'S NOT AS IF THERE'S ANYTHING TO SEE.

YOU FORGOT TO LOCK IT. HEY, WHAT'S THAT? SINCE WHEN DO YOU NEED A BRA?

YOU THINK YOU'RE SO FUNNY. WHY DON'T YOU GO AND SQUEEZE A SPOT?

△ Suzanne told Jeremy to get out, but he just laughed.

▷ Mrs Green had heard them arguing. She had come upstairs and told Jeremy to stop teasing his sister.

A COUPLE OF YEARS AGO, WE COULDN'T GET YOU OUT OF THE BATHROOM EITHER, AND I'M NOT GOING TO BEGIN TO ASK WHAT YOU WERE DOING.

AW, MUM, LEAVE IT OUT!

▽ Mrs Green and Suzanne talked together for a while.

YOU CAN'T RUSH THESE THINGS, YOU KNOW. EVERYBODY DEVELOPS AT THEIR OWN PACE.

▽ Jeremy went back to his room. Suzanne tried on her new bra.

HE'S RIGHT, THOUGH, MUM. SOME OF THE OTHER GIRLS AT SCHOOL ARE MUCH BIGGER THAN I AM.

I WOULDN'T WORRY ABOUT THAT. THERE ARE ALL SORTS OF DIFFERENT BODIES. WE CAN'T ALL BE THE SAME.

WELL I WISH I'D HURRY UP!

11

▽ The next day, after school, Suzanne called round to her friend Alex's house.

> ARE YOU OKAY? I WAS WORRIED ABOUT YOU WHEN YOU DIDN'T COME TO SCHOOL TODAY.

> I'LL TELL YOU INSIDE.

▽ Alex explained that she had had her first period that morning.

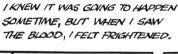

> I KNEW IT WAS GOING TO HAPPEN SOMETIME, BUT WHEN I SAW THE BLOOD, I FELT FRIGHTENED.

> DIDN'T YOUR MUM TALK TO YOU ABOUT IT BEFOREHAND?

> A BIT, BUT MUM AND DAD GET EMBARRASSED TALKING ABOUT THINGS LIKE THAT.

△ Alex told Suzanne that she only knew what she had learnt at school.

▽ Suzanne was surprised.

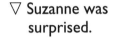

> MUM TOLD ME ALL ABOUT IT, SO WHEN I STARTED, I KNEW WHAT TO EXPECT. THERE'S NOTHING TO BE AFRAID OF. HAVE YOU USED A SANITARY TOWEL?

> YES. I TOOK ONE OF MUM'S.

▽ Suzanne told Alex that she should tell her mum about it.

> I WAS LOOKING FORWARD TO GOING DANCING TOMORROW, AND NOW I WON'T BE ABLE TO.

> WHY NOT? JUST BECAUSE YOU'VE GOT YOUR PERIOD, THAT DOESN'T MEAN YOU HAVE TO STOP DOING THINGS.

▽ The next evening, Alex did go to the school disco.

> I SPOKE TO MUM, LIKE YOU SAID, AND TOLD HER WHAT HAD HAPPENED. SHE WAS REALLY GOOD IN THE END, AND WE HAD A LONG TALK ABOUT IT.

> SHE WAS JUST EMBARRASSED BEFORE. DAD STILL GETS RED-FACED WHEN HE TALKS TO MATTHEW AND ME ABOUT PERSONAL STUFF.

BREAST DEVELOPMENT VARIES FROM PERSON TO PERSON, AS SUZANNE HAS DISCOVERED.

It is quite normal for one breast to grow at a slower rate than the other. This will eventually balance out, although it is common for one breast to remain slightly larger than the other. Whatever size you become, you will need to choose the right size of bra for you.

IT IS IMPORTANT TO USE A PAD OR TAMPON WHEN HAVING A PERIOD.

It is a good idea to try out the different methods available to find the one you feel most comfortable with. Sanitary towels can be held in place with a belt, or they can be stuck to ordinary pants. Tampons can be used with or without an applicator. Pads and tampons should be changed frequently for reasons of hygiene and health.

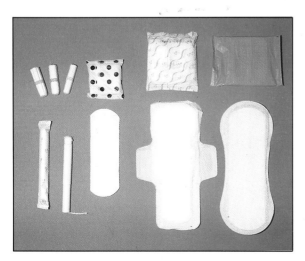

FACT FILE: PERIODS

A few months before your first period, you may feel some stomach pains. A small amount of milky discharge from the vagina is another sign that your period may be starting soon. The first period can be worrying, especially if you have not been told what to expect. Periods usually happen once a month but at first they may not come on time, or when you expect them. You may even miss one or two. Some people feel discomfort during their period – back ache and/or stomach cramps. Some people may also experience mood swings before a period. This is called pre-menstrual syndrome and is due to changes in hormone levels. Many people will feel no discomfort. A period need not get in the way of enjoying everyday physical activities.

–5– Physical Changes In Boys

Puberty usually begins later in boys than in girls, and it often takes longer.

For boys, some of the first physical signs that puberty has begun are the growth of the penis and testicles. The testicles begin to produce sperm, the male sex cells. Boys may also notice the appearance of facial and body hair. Hair usually grows around the penis and testicles, and under the arms. As they get older, some boys also grow hair on their chest and other parts of their body.

Boys may well see a gradual increase in the amount of facial hair, but at first this may be very soft, and they may not need to shave regularly until they are older. The vocal chords also change, making most boys' voices deeper. This can take a while, and for a time the voice may become husky or squeaky before it 'breaks' properly. Some boys may find that their nipples become sore and slightly swollen. If so, this tenderness will disappear in time.

In many boys, there is a sharp spurt in overall body growth. Some can grow up to four inches in height in as many months. The chest will grow broader, and there will be an increase, however gradual, in muscle.

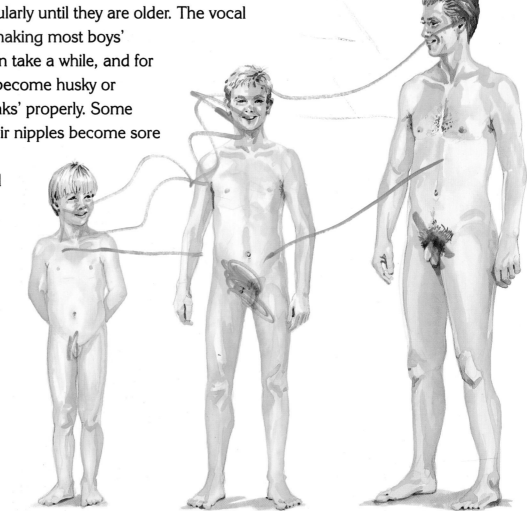

14

▽ A few weeks later, Fran and Tony and their new baby, Paul, had come round for a meal.

▽ After the meal, Matt offered to help Tony clear up in the kitchen.

WHAT BROUGHT THIS ON? SINCE WHEN HAVE YOU HELPED AROUND THE HOUSE?

ARE YOU ALRIGHT? YOU SEEM VERY QUIET.

JUST LEAVE ME ALONE.

I JUST WANT TO ASK TONY SOMETHING, THAT'S ALL.

▷ In the kitchen, Matt closed the door, so nobody would hear their conversation.

YOU SEEM TO HAVE SOMETHING ON YOUR MIND. DO YOU WANT TO TELL ME ABOUT IT?

▽ Tony said that he was still only a medical student, but would do his best to help.

WELL, IT'S REALLY EMBARRASSING. WE'VE BEEN HAVING THESE TALKS ABOUT PUBERTY, AND NOW I'M WORRIED IN CASE I'M NOT NORMAL.

WELL, I KNOW I COULD TALK TO DAD, BUT SINCE YOU'RE A DOCTOR I THOUGHT YOU'D BE THE BEST PERSON TO ASK.

▽ Matt said that he had noticed that some of his friends seemed to be more developed than he was.

I DOUBT IT. IT'S SOMETHING LOTS OF BOYS WORRY ABOUT WHEN THEY'RE GROWING UP, AND THE TEASING DOESN'T HELP.

SOME OF THEM TEASED ME. DO YOU THINK I MIGHT NOT BE GROWING PROPERLY?

THERE'S NOTHING TO BE EMBARRASSED ABOUT. WHAT'S BOTHERING YOU?

△ The two of them talked for a while. Tony was able to put Matt's mind at rest.

15

▽ Tony said that he remembered what it was like when he was twelve years old, with all these changes happening.

I KEEP HAVING THESE FEELINGS I'VE NEVER HAD BEFORE.

IT SEEMS LIKE YOUR BODY HAS A MIND OF ITS OWN, DOESN'T IT?

I KNOW. AS IF THE PHYSICAL CHANGES WEREN'T ENOUGH, SUDDENLY YOUR EMOTIONS START TO GO HAYWIRE. IT'S ALL PERFECTLY NORMAL, MATT. IT JUST TAKES A BIT OF GETTING USED TO.

YOU CAN SAY THAT AGAIN. I KEEP BURSTING INTO TEARS FOR NO REASON.

△ Matt was pleased he had decided to confide in Tony.

▽ A couple of days later, Matt and Saheed saw Adam writing secretively in the playground.

WHAT ARE YOU UP TO?

IT'S NONE OF YOUR BUSINESS. IT'S PRIVATE.

▽ Saheed grabbed the piece of paper that Adam had been writing on and held it out of his reach.

IT'S A QUESTION FOR MR BUCKLEY'S SUGGESTION BOX. HE WANTS TO KNOW IF WET DREAMS ARE NORMAL.

GIVE ME THAT.

▽ Even Saheed began to laugh. Suzanne and her friends pointed to them.

GIVE IT BACK TO HIM, SAHEED. IT'S MEANT TO BE PRIVATE. SORRY, ADAM.

ME TOO, ADAM. WHAT'S A WET DREAM ANYWAY?

I CAN'T BELIEVE WE'RE THE SAME AGE. THEY'RE SO CHILDISH.

△ Matt and Adam looked at Saheed, and suddenly burst out laughing.

LIKE MATT, MANY BOYS WORRY ABOUT THE SIZE OF THEIR PENIS.
This can sometimes make them feel very self-conscious. It is also often the cause of teasing and jokes amongst boys. But remember that whatever size you are, or become, the size of the penis is not related to its function. All boys have erections. When you get an erection, more blood flows into the tissues of the penis, and the muscles at the base of the penis contract. This causes it to become stiffer and longer.

DURING PUBERTY IT IS COMMON FOR THE BODY TO PLAY PHYSICAL AS WELL AS EMOTIONAL TRICKS.
Boys going through puberty may have erections more frequently than they used to. These can often be when you least expect, or want them. Although you may sometimes be embarrassed about it, it is a perfectly normal part of the growing up process.

THE ANSWER TO ADAM'S QUESTION.
Yes. Most boys going through puberty will experience 'wet dreams', and they are nothing to worry about. The body can store only a limited amount of sperm. Getting rid of unused sperm during sleep, often accompanied by sexy dreams, is quite natural.

– 6 – Looking After Yourself

Growing up means learning how to look after yourself, both physically and emotionally.

You are only given one body – and it is yours for life. It is important that you are familiar with it, understand how it works, and know how to take care of it. This is especially true during puberty, when changes which you have not experienced before can be very confusing, and can sometimes make you wonder whether your body really is your own!

Growing up might mean accepting things like wearing braces to make sure your teeth are straight and stay that way. This can be hard to accept, particularly if others make fun of you. This is why it is worth thinking about things in the long term.

With the sudden growth spurt, many young people find themselves becoming clumsy. This usually passes, but getting used to all of this 'new you' can take time. During puberty, washing and general hygiene become more important, as the skin produces more grease and the body begins to sweat more.

As they get older, girls and women should check their breasts regularly, to make sure that there are no unusual lumps. Boys and men should do the same to their testicles. Self-examination can mean that any potential problems are spotted early and dealt with. If you do have any doubts about any aspect of your health, it is a good idea to talk to someone about your concerns.

A WEEK LATER...

WHAT ON EARTH WAS THAT ALL ABOUT? WE COULD HEAR YOU TWO ARGUING IN HERE.

IT MUST BE THAT TIME OF THE MONTH.

▽ That evening, Jeremy was getting ready to go out. His friend, Chris, had called round for him.

IF YOU DON'T HURRY UP, THE GIRLS WILL THINK WE'RE NOT COMING.

THAT SHOWS HOW MUCH YOU KNOW. I HATE THAT ALEX. SHE'S SUCH A LIAR—ALWAYS BRAGGING ABOUT SOME NEW BOYFRIEND OR OTHER. I'M NEVER GOING TO SPEAK TO HER AGAIN.

GREAT. MY FIRST DATE WITH SARAH, AND I'VE GOT A FACE LIKE A PEPPERONI PIZZA.

△ Suzanne ran upstairs to her room.

▽ Suzanne knocked on the door, and came in.

HI, CHRIS. I THOUGHT I HEARD YOU ARRIVE. I LIKE YOUR JACKET.

YOU'RE NOT GOING OUT IN THAT OLD SHIRT, ARE YOU? YOU'VE HAD IT ON FOR DAYS.

IT'S MY FAVOURITE. ANYHOW, WHO ASKED YOU TO COME IN? GO AND PLAY WITH YOUR TOYS.

THANKS, I JUST BOUGHT IT.

WELL, THE SMELL ALONE'S KNOCKING ME OUT. URGH, YOU STINK.

I HATE TO TELL YOU, MATE, BUT SHE'S RIGHT. YOU ARE A BIT...WHIFFY.

I THOUGHT YOU TWO WEREN'T SPEAKING. WHAT HAPPENED?

OH, THAT WAS NOTHING. LOOK, SUZANNE—HE'S THE ONE, ISN'T HE SEXY?

◁ Jeremy decided to change his shirt.

▷ Two days later, Mrs Green found Suzanne and Alex chatting in the kitchen.

NOT BAD, BUT HE'S MORE MY TYPE. HE LOOKS JUST LIKE CHRIS.

JEREMY KNOWS THAT ACNE CAN BE A PARTICULAR PROBLEM.

Good hygiene is important but the problem is not about how well you wash. Although there are many creams and lotions available, there is no one quick cure for acne. Some people find sunshine helps. It is important not to squeeze or pick spots, however much you might want to. This can spread the infection and leave scars. Pubertal acne usually fades in a person's late teens.

DURING PUBERTY, THE SMELL OF SWEAT MAY BE STRONGER THAN BEFORE.

This is natural, but it does mean being aware of hygiene. Deodorants and frequent washing can help. It is important to change clothes regularly, as the smell can stay on them, and become stale.

PUBERTY IS A TIME OF INTENSE AND SOMETIMES MIXED UP EMOTIONS.

Within a few days, Suzanne and Alex have been best friends, had a major argument and become best friends again.

Mood swings – sudden dramatic changes in your feelings – are common when growing up. But as Suzanne has pointed out, they do not necessarily have anything to do with a girl's menstrual cycle. Both boys and girls can be affected by unexpected moods swings. You may go from feeling very shy and self-conscious one moment, to feeling quite confident the next. This can be very puzzling and upsetting, but it helps to remember that lots of people feel like this.

−7− *Handling Emotional Changes*

Although the physical changes of puberty are not always easy to cope with, they do at least follow a more or less set pattern. However, the emotional side is not so easy to predict. Certainly there will be new feelings to experience but it can also be a time of doubt and confusion. Puberty may make you question values and attitudes which, up until now, you may have been quite happy with. Your emotions may be much more intense than they used to be.

Clashes with parents and carers are common during puberty. Everyone may need to learn to give and take a little.

Chief amongst the new feelings will be sexual attraction. You may begin to feel 'sexy' yourself, and may start to fantasise about other people. There is nothing wrong with this but it may not always be appropriate to express these feelings to others. Just as it takes time for the body to adapt completely to physical changes, it takes a while to come to terms with these new feelings and to understand them fully.

As you begin to have a sense of being 'grown up', you may find yourself disagreeing with other people's ideas about your behaviour. Even close relationships can come under pressure. It is not unusual for there to be more tension between girls and boys, who may at one time have been good friends. In the heat of the moment, boys and girls sometimes say hurtful things to each other. Growing up sometimes means growing apart from people we were once close to.

Handling Emotional Changes

▽ One evening, six weeks later, Michelle and Alex called for Suzanne. Alex's brother was taking them to a pop concert.

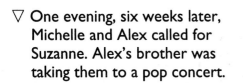

HI, WELCOME TO THE WAR ZONE. YOU LOOK NICE TONIGHT, ALEX. I DON'T THINK I'VE EVER SEEN YOU IN MAKE UP.

HEY, ALEX. I THINK HE FANCIES YOU.

DON'T BE SILLY. WHAT'S GOING ON MATT?

▽ Matt explained that his parents were upset because Suzanne had cut and dyed her hair without telling them.

I DON'T KNOW WHAT YOU'RE SO UPSET ABOUT. CHRIS SAID IT SUITED ME. HE LIKES GIRLS WITH SHORT HAIR.

YOU ARE NOT GOING OUT LOOKING LIKE THAT. I DON'T CARE WHAT CHRIS LIKES. AND HE'S TOO OLD FOR YOU, YOUNG LADY.

▽ Suzanne refused to listen. She said her mum and dad didn't understand.

SUZANNE, WE WOULDN'T HAVE MINDED, BUT YOU SHOULD HAVE DISCUSSED IT WITH US FIRST.

WHY? WHY CAN'T I MAKE MY OWN DECISIONS? IT'S NOT FAIR.

▽ Suzanne stormed off to the concert. Matt went back upstairs, where he had been listening to music with Saheed and Adam. He had something to show them.

WOW, LOOK SAHEED. MATTHEW, WHERE DID YOU GET THIS?

IN JEREMY'S ROOM. HE'S GOT A WHOLE PILE OF THEM HIDDEN IN THERE.

▽ Jeremy had heard the boys giggling. He came into Matt's room and snatched up the magazine before storming out.

I'LL TAKE THAT, THANK YOU. AND I'M GOING TO TELL MUM WHAT YOU WERE ALL DOING.

GO ON THEN. I'LL JUST TELL HER WHERE THE MAGAZINE CAME FROM—AND ABOUT THE OTHERS YOU'VE GOT.

▽ Later, Suzanne came back from the concert, feeling a little guilty.

THE CONCERT WAS GREAT. AND I'M SORRY ABOUT EARLIER.

JUST GO TO BED NOW, SUZANNE. WE'LL TALK ABOUT IT TOMORROW.

SUZANNE HAS A CRUSH ON CHRIS.
Crushes are periods of intense emotional or physical attraction to another person – perhaps to someone you know, or to a pop, TV or film star. They are perfectly normal, especially during puberty. You may have a crush on somebody much older than you are. You may feel strongly about someone of the same sex – this does not necessarily mean that you are homosexual. Keeping your feelings a secret can make them even more intense. Crushes usually pass with time.

PUBERTY CAN BE A TIME OF TRYING TO WORK OUT WHERE YOU BELONG IN THE WORLD.
So many changes happen during puberty, that at times it can feel as if you are a totally different person. Many people go through various phases and may hold different ideas and attitudes as they grow up.

FACT FILE: MASTURBATION

Masturbation means rubbing or playing with your sexual organs. Both sexes enjoy masturbation, and most people do it, or have done at some time in their lives. Masturbation usually involves some form of sexual fantasy. Some people and cultures have strong feelings about it. But despite what you may have heard, it is not a 'dirty' habit, and can do you no harm. It is a way of exploring your own body, and dealing with natural sexual urges. It is important to choose an appropriate, private place.

—8— *Responsibilities*

Part of growing up is about taking responsibility for yourself and your behaviour. Responsible behaviour often means different things to different people but it involves developing a sense of respect for yourself and for others. Decision-making is not always easy. With the freedom to decide for yourself comes the need to understand that others may not agree with you, and to accept that sometimes you might make the wrong decision.

As you grow older, you may resent having to do what parents or other older adults tell you to. You may feel that you are old enough to decide for yourself. Parents and carers can often find it hard to accept that you are no longer the child you once were. They are trying to get used to the changes in you too.

Sex is an exciting and pleasurable part of many grown up people's lives. It is a subject most young people will start to think more about as they grow older. There is nothing wrong with this. But just because your body is physically capable of having sex, does not mean that you will be emotionally ready for it. There are laws which lay down the ages at which young people can have sex.

As you grow up, you will often be given more opportunity to make decisions for yourself. If you make a promise – for instance to be home by a certain time – it is your responsibility to keep to it.

3 MONTHS LATER...

HERE YOU ARE. SORRY TO BREAK IN ON YOU LOVEBIRDS. I CALLED FOR YOU THIS MORNING MATT, BUT YOUR MUM SAID YOU'D ALREADY LEFT.

HAVE YOU HEARD ABOUT JIMMY'S SISTER? SHE'S PREGNANT. SHE'S GOING TO HAVE TO LEAVE SCHOOL AND EVERYTHING.

I DON'T BELIEVE IT. WHO'S THE FATHER?

I WALKED TO SCHOOL WITH ALEX TODAY, THAT'S ALL.

△ Adam had started to make fun of them, but was interrupted by Michelle.

I DON'T KNOW, BUT I THINK IT'S AWFUL, ANYWAY. SHE SHOULD HAVE KNOWN BETTER.

DO YOU EVER THINK ABOUT WHAT SEX IS LIKE?

△ Suzanne said she thought it was just as much the boy's responsibility.

IT'S NOT ALL HER FAULT. SHE DIDN'T GET PREGNANT ON HER OWN, AFTER ALL.

I THINK EVERYBODY THINKS ABOUT IT, SOMETIMES. THAT'S NO REASON TO RUSH INTO ANYTHING THOUGH.

HAVE A GOOD TIME, JEREMY—BUT NOT TOO GOOD, IF YOU KNOW WHAT I MEAN. I'M NOT SURE ABOUT THIS CHRIS PERSON. I HOPE I CAN TRUST YOU NOT TO DO ANYTHING SILLY.

I KNOW, BUT THESE DAYS YOU HAVE TO BE CAREFUL. JUST BE SENSIBLE, THAT'S ALL.

I WILL, DON'T WORRY. NOW I'VE GOT TO GO, OR I'LL BE LATE PICKING UP SARAH.

CHRIS IS OK. IT'S JUST A PARTY, DAD, NOTHING WILD, I PROMISE.

△ That evening, as Jeremy was going to Chris's party, Mr Green thought that growing up was just as hard on the parents as the children.

EXPERIMENTATION IS A NATURAL PART OF GROWING UP.

Feeling curious about new experiences is normal. This does not mean you have to rush into anything. There can be a lot of pressure from friends and other people to try new things, such as drugs, or sex.

Being responsible means recognising the dangers of experimentation. You should not feel pressurised into doing anything you are unhappy about.

MOST PEOPLE EXPECT TO ENJOY AN INTIMATE RELATIONSHIP AT SOME POINT IN THEIR LIVES.

There is no rule which says you have to have a boyfriend or girlfriend at any particular time. Having one, or pretending to, just to impress others, is not a good idea. Forming an intimate relationship is not a step to be taken lightly.

FACT FILE:
SEX AND RELATIONSHIPS

Responsible partners will consider the physical and emotional issues involved, before starting a sexual relationship. You may have heard of safer sex. Sex is not dangerous, but using condoms can reduce the risk of infection from HIV – the virus which can lead to AIDS. They are also one of many forms of contraceptive. Contraception is the responsibility of both the man and the woman. The first sexual experience is not something which should be rushed into.

—9— *Am I Grown Up Now?*

Many young people cannot wait to grow up. Even very young children will play at being adults. However, it is not a process to be rushed. There may be no exact point at which you will suddenly know that you are 'grown up'. Everyone develops at his or her own pace. There is, however, an age at which you will be legally treated as an adult.

By trying to grow up too fast, you might be missing out on some of the experiences which childhood has to offer.

As you grow older, your expectations of yourselves and other people will change. You may come to think that a younger brother or sister is now very childish. You may feel that older adults do not understand what you are going through. For their part, they may be having trouble accepting you as a young person with your own viewpoints.

There is plenty of time to enjoy the many new experiences which lie ahead of you. The years we spend as children often enrich our adult lives. As you grow up, you might feel a lot of pressure on you to behave in a certain way. But learning to trust your instincts and to believe in yourself will help you to make the right decisions.

△ It was Matt and Suzanne's birthday. Tony and Fran had come round with their presents.

SO HOW'S EVERYTHING MATT? ANY MORE WORRIES?

IT'S JUST WHAT I WANTED.

NO. I DON'T THINK I'LL EVER START SHAVING, BUT OTHERWISE EVERYTHING'S FINE. IT'S GREAT HAVING YOU TO TALK TO - THANKS FOR ALL YOUR ADVICE.

△ Later, Matt and Suzanne were getting ready for their party that evening.

I DO HOPE THE MUSIC ISN'T GOING TO BE TOO LOUD. AND WHERE ARE YOUR FATHER AND I SUPPOSED TO SIT?

YOU DON'T MEAN YOU'RE GOING TO BE HERE! BUT MUM, ALL OUR FRIENDS ARE COMING.

WE'LL BE A LAUGHING STOCK. NO-ONE HAS THEIR PARENTS AT A PARTY.

△ Mrs Green laughed and told them she was only joking.

DON'T WORRY. WE'LL KEEP OUT OF YOUR WAY, AS LONG AS JEREMY'S HERE. JEREMY YOU ARE STAYING FOR THE PARTY, AREN'T YOU?

IF I HAVE TO. AS LONG AS THEY DON'T BOTHER ME. SARAH'S COMING ROUND.

I THINK HE'S MADE HER UP. HE HASN'T REALLY GOT A GIRLFRIEND.

SO ARE WE GOING TO MEET THE MYSTERIOUS SARAH? SHE'S ALL YOU TALK ABOUT THESE DAYS.

YOU'RE THE ONE WHO'LL NEVER GET A GIRLFRIEND, WIMP! WE JUST WANT TO SPEND SOME TIME ON OUR OWN.

△ An hour later, Sarah arrived and Jeremy introduced her to his parents.

SHE'S ALRIGHT I SUPPOSE.

SHE SEEMS REALLY NICE. I HOPE YOU PREPARED HER FOR MUM AND DAD.

DON'T WORRY. I'VE TOLD HER ALL ABOUT THEM. AND ABOUT YOU TWO - SO NO MESSING ABOUT, OK?

THAT EVENING...

HOW COME YOU'VE BEEN DANCING WITH ADAM'S BROTHER ALL NIGHT? I THOUGHT YOU FANCIED CHRIS.

NO, THAT WAS AGES AGO. SHE'S BEEN MAD ABOUT DAVE FOR WEEKS NOW.

I DO HAVE MY OWN LIFE YOU KNOW. WE'RE NOT KIDS ANY MORE.

△ Laughing, they all went to join their friends.

MATT HAS FOUND THAT IT HAS HELPED HIM TO HAVE TONY TO TALK TO.

Finding someone you trust to discuss your feelings and anxieties with, can help at many times in our lives. During puberty, you may feel that your parents or carers do not understand what you are going through. Their ideas may seem old-fashioned or restrictive, especially if you are trying to find your own identity. Remember, though, that they experienced the same kinds of feelings when they were your age. They were young once! It can also help to talk openly to your friends – they may well be feeling just the same as you.

RELATIONSHIPS DO NOT ALWAYS STAY THE SAME.

Even though Matt and Suzanne are still close, they do not always want to share everything that is happening in their lives. Privacy can be particularly important during puberty, especially if you are trying to come to terms with new emotions. You may feel you want space by yourself, and you will need to make sure people understand this.

WITH ALL THE CHANGES THAT HAPPEN DURING PUBERTY, IT IS EASY TO FORGET THAT GROWING UP CAN ALSO BE FUN!

Many cultures celebrate the changes. Some have ceremonies that mark the end of child-hood. Growing up is not all difficult. There is much to enjoy and to feel good about.

What Can We Do?

Puberty is an exciting part of each person's life. Like everything else, it has its ups and downs. Although we all go through similar changes and experience some of the same feelings and concerns, the actual experience of growing up will be different for each person. Having read this book, you will understand more about the effects that puberty can have on your life.

"It helps knowing that everyone goes through puberty, and that what I feel is normal."

If you have started puberty already, allow yourself to enjoy it. If you have not yet started, don't worry – there is no given age at which it begins.

Adults sometimes forget that young people may be sensitive about the changes which are happening to them. Trying to remember how they felt when they were going through puberty may help them to understand how you are feeling now.

If you are unsure about anything, or if you have any particular worries, remember that talking to somebody can often help to put your mind at ease.

As you become a young adult, there will be a lot to come to terms with. But growing up and discovering new experiences can be great fun.

Adults and children who have read this book together may like to discuss their feelings about the issues involved. Anybody who would like to talk to someone, not directly involved, about any aspect of puberty, may be able to obtain information, support or advice from the organisations listed below.

CHILDLINE
50 Studd Street
London
N1 OQW
Tel: 0207 239 1000
Tel: 0800 1111(helpline)
E-mail:
reception@childline.org.uk

THE CHILDREN'S SOCIETY
56-89 Margery Street
London
WC1X OJL
Tel: 0207 837 4299
Website:
www.the-childrens-society.org.uk

BROOK ADVISORY CENTRES
165 Gray's Inn Road
London
WC1X 8UD
Tel: 0207 708 1234
Tel: 0207 617 8000 (helpline)

THE NATIONAL ASSOCIATION OF CITIZENS' ADVICE BUREAUX
115 Pentonville Road
London
N1 9LZ
Tel: 0207 833 2181 for details of your nearest branch

MINISTRY OF YOUTH
PO Box 10-300
Wellington
New Zealand
Tel: 00 644 471 2158

DEPARTMENT OF HEALTH
Richmond House
79 Whitehall
London
SW1A 2NS
Tel: 0800 665544 (health information service)
Tel: 0800 555777 (health literature line)

NATIONAL YOUTH FOUNDATION
P.O. Box 606
Carlingford
New South Wales
2118
Australia
Tel: 00 612 211 1788

Index

Photocredits

All the pictures in this book are by Roger Vlitos apart from page 26, top, Frank Spooner Pictures. The publishers wish to acknowledge that all the people photographed in this book are models.